UNDERSTANDING THE WILL OF GOD FOR YOUR LIFE

ALAN L. CHESTER

The events and dialogues recorded in this literary work are based on the recollections of Alan L. Chester. Specific names, details, dates, and geographical information have been excluded in order to reserve certain individuals' rights to privacy

Understanding the Will of God For Your Life © 2018
by
Alan L. Chester

Printed in the United States of America.

ISBN-13: 978-1984204196

ISBN-10: 198420419X

First Edition: January 2018

CONTENTS

Dedication

This book is dedicated to my wife, Dr. Shanta L. Chester. Thank you for inspiring me to begin writing again. Your love and patience have renewed my hope and faith in the greatness of God within me. To our children, grandchildren and godchildren, I love you all with all of my heart. To my mother, Doris Chester, thank you for introducing me to the Name of Jesus. I miss you so much. To my sister, Dr. Sylvia James, thank you for believing in me when I did not even believe in myself. To my father, Lewis Gittings, who showed me unconditional love. To my brother, Steven Chester, I love you, Bro. To my mother-in-law and my father-in-law, Elder Joseph and Sis. Rosetta Stevens, thank you for your love and prayers that helped to cover me. To my spiritual sons and daughters of Fresh Fire Ministries, I am so grateful for your prayers and commitment that keep me encouraged. To the Bishops and Pastors, who pray for me, I love you as my brothers. Last but not least, to the King of kings and the Lord of lords, who saved me from death, hell, and the grave, Jesus Christ. Thank you Father for teaching me that there is no safer place than in the will of God.

PREFACE

In this great country that we live in called

America, there are over 250,000 Christian churches

and over 100,000 different denominations. We are

home to some of the greatest preachers and teachers

within the last 100 years. Yet, it is thought by some,

that many are leaving the local church either to stay

home on Sundays and sleep-in or to explore other

religions such as Islam, Buddhism or Christian

Science. In my opinion, the Church of our Lord Jesus

Christ is growing stronger every day. There are

revivals breaking out both near and far. People are

being saved in Africa, Asia, and Europe through the

introduction of the love of God through Jesus Christ.

In this day and time, church attendance may be

considered popular by those of a certain status; those

who seek to gain political or financial gain and even

by those who only seem to enjoy the music and the

bright lights. In some circles, this may be an

acceptable practice, but Jesus is not returning to

rapture a popular people; those who are musically

talented, or a highly, entertaining Church. Instead, He

is returning for a church that knows their God and

have a desire to do His will (Dan. 11:32, King James

Version (KJV)).

In I John 2:21 (KJV), the Apostle John writes to

the church, "I have not written unto you because ye

know not the truth, but because ye know it, and that

no lie is in the truth" (I John 2:21, KJV). In this text,

John is saying that he is not writing to you because

you are ignorant or blind to the things of God, but

because you know…you understand. God wants us to know and not to live in doubt and fear over what we call the unknown or uncertainty of things to come. The Lord spoke through the prophet, Hosea, saying: "My people are destroyed for lack of knowledge…" (Hosea 4:6, KJV). So in reality, not knowing is the ultimate enemy. There is no bliss in ignorance or not knowing.

Not knowing will lead the Child of God down a road blindly, with the possibility of falling into a ditch (Matt. 15:14, KJV). The ditch is not a detour, but a dead end, that is miles away from your destiny, your purpose, and your place in God. So many good people are entering the doors of the church, Sunday after Sunday, informed of God but not knowing the God that they have just heard preached about.

The Webster Dictionary defines the

word *knowledge* as "the fact or condition of knowing something with familiarity, which is gained through experience or association" (2013). We must become more familiar with God by experience if we are going to know Him in an intimate way. What God has done for others is wonderful to hear about. For instance, who isn't encouraged to hear the testimony of Daniel being delivered from a lion's den or about David gaining the victory over Goliath. These are truly testaments as to the divine power of our God, but you cannot gain victories in your own life by other people's testimonies alone. There must come a time when you experience God's power for yourself.

It is through your daily encounters with God that help you to understand who He is and what His will is for your life. We can't just know Him as the God of Abraham, or the God of Paul or our grandmother's God, but we must know Him as OUR God and Lord in order to live a life filled with the blessings that He can provide. It is not wise to think that you can live your life as you please and to rise into Heaven on grandma's testimony. Oh no, my friend, there will be *no hitchhiking into Heaven*; no riding on your preacher's coattail, or your mama's apron strings. We must know our God and know His will for our lives for ourselves.

So, as we walk through these pages

together to understand the will of God for our lives,

let us not prophesy to our neighbor concerning the

will of God for *their* lives, but let us search the mind

of God to find out what He desires for you and I;

personally. Let us refuse to walk into the church,

Sunday after Sunday, feeling lost. In other words, let

us not experience being born-again, but still appear

lost in our daily living because we have no idea

where God wants us to go or what in the world He

wants us to do; No...not in this season. Instead, let us

boldly declare that we will know the God that we

sing about. Let us empathically declare that we will

draw closer to Him, so that we will understand what

His will is for our lives.

APPLICATION EXERCISE:

Write down 5 things that you would love to ask God about because you just honestly do not understand. (For example, maybe you desire to seek understanding about a very difficult time in your life that you've encountered.) Pray what you wrote down back to God. Then, wait patiently and the Lord will reveal His will.

1. _____

_____

2. _____

_____

3. _____

_____

4. _____

_____

5. _____

_____

1

THE PERFECT WILL OF GOD

Understanding the will of God is very simplistic yet, it is also very profound. The will of God cannot actually be studied; it must be experienced. God is so loving and engaging that He has no desire to force His will upon those that have no desire to allow Him to perform it. Theoretically, God rules and reigns in Heaven and on Earth, yet, He allows mankind to choose what master they will serve. Whether we choose to serve good or whether we choose to serve evil, God loves us so much that He gives us the right to decide as Jesus did by saying "…not my will but your will be done" (Luke 22:42, KJV).

Not only can the will of God not be studied but it cannot be understood by human intellect. Man's intellect is limited to his experiences. As an individual, we can assume that we know what is best for ourselves based on what we've gone through or witnessed others go through. This is a common practice of mankind. However, it is problematic because we don't always know what's best for ourselves. That's why we don't always make decisions that result in positive outcomes. The truth of the matter is, that our ability to think ourselves into or out of a situation is flawed by our sinful nature that only desires what looks good, what taste good, what feels good, what sounds good or what smells good. Our natural senses consist of sight, sound, smell, touch, and taste. It is through our senses that we connect to our natural world, but the will of God connects us to a spiritual world in which our senses have no real point of reference. It is no wonder that the scriptures tell us to "… lean not to our own understanding…" (Proverbs 3:5, KJV) because what makes sense to God, makes no sense to our human intellect.

I Corinthians 2:14 (KJV) teaches us that spiritual things must be compared to spiritual things, and that the natural man has no comprehension of God's will (I Corinthians 2:14, KJV). This text clearly explains why we cannot rely on human intellect. Therefore, our spiritual man must seek the mind of God to gain understanding and direction. As far as our natural thinking, we struggle to comprehend the supernatural. Yet, God uses our natural experiences to create supernatural moments. These moments give God the opportunity He needs to perform His will in the lives of His children. So, in actuality, the will of the Lord is done without prohibiting man from making his own choices. For it is through our relationship with Christ, that we learn the significance of striking a balance between the perfect will of God and what some may call the permissive will of God. Let's visit this theoretical understanding to gain enlightenment.

In many Christian schools of thought and theological modes of thinking, the will of God is sometimes said to be revealed in a dual manner. It is argued that there are two ways to view the will of God: permissive will and perfect will.

When we look at the perfect will of God, we can clearly see a divine plan that was predetermined in the mind of God. 1 Thessalonians 5:18 (KJV) says: "In everything give thanks: for this is the will of God in Christ Jesus concerning you." So, through this scripture, we must understand that there is a reason to thank God in everything that we go through. We should remember that all things established from the mind of God were spoken out of His mouth and that word that is spoken, unfolds in the lives of the people of God. The Bible shares with us that God is omniscient or He knows all things. So, we can say because God is omniscient and knows all things, that the daily affairs of mankind are divinely orchestrated by the sovereign hand of God. No problem is too big or too small for God to intervene in so that He can assist in our success. Yet, we often do not give God the opportunity because we want to rule our own destiny, since we are free to make our own decisions. The Lord allows us to be chastened by our bad choices. Once we make choices that take us out of His perfect will, the consequences of our actions reveal what God permitted or in other words, His permissive will becomes clearly evident. The consequences of our bad choices may be what God permitted however, our obedience to His Word will only reveal His perfect will.

APPLICATION EXERCISE:

Have you ever made a bad decision in your past that you are still suffering from the consequences of today? Think about some of the bad choices you've made. As you reflect, don't blame God or anyone else for these decisions. Hold yourself accountable.

 Write down the five bad decisions that you've made that are still affecting you today. Then, pray and ask God to heal you from the consequences of these decisions.

1. _____

_____

2. _____

_____

3. _____

_____

4. _____

_____

5. _____

_____

2

DEFINING THE PERFECT WILL OF GOD

Webster (2013) defines *perfect* as "being without fault or defect; exact, precise, complete, relating to … an action or state completed at the time of speaking… or time spoken of." When it comes to the will of God, there is no gray area, His will is precise, without fault or defect. In fact, it is complete all by itself. God is not wishy-washy. He's not guessing, assuming, nor contemplating His next move, but He is absolute in His thinking. Based on His precision of knowing, there is nothing that you or I can face that our God is not aware of. If He's numbered the hairs on our heads by number and knows them by the digit that they're numbered, then how much more does He recognize our daily fight with life's experience?

In Ephesians 1:11 (KJV), it reads: "In whom also we have obtained an inheritance, being predestinated according to the purpose of Him who works all things after the counsel of His own will..." This scripture declares to us that the Lord doesn't have to call a meeting of the minds to determine the best course of action for His creation. No, but the Father predetermines our purpose after the counsel of His own will. He already knows the end from the beginning (Isa. 46:10, KJV). In other words, He's read the book before He even wrote it. He determined in His mind His perfect will and by the power of His word, His will was, is, and will continue to be

performed.

The word *perfect* is defined as "a verb tense

that expresses an action or state completed at the time

of speaking or a time spoken." Therefore, the perfect

will of God was established in creation when the Lord

spoke it. When God said it, His word took action and

nothing could prevent or hinder His word from

accomplishing what He sent it to do. David said in

Psalms 119:89 (AMP): "... O Lord, thy Word is settled

in heaven." In the Amplified Bible this same verse

reads: "Thy word stands firm in heaven." From the

moment the Lord said "...let there be..." there was,

there has been, and always will be. The sun rises,

from our perspective, because we see it from our

point of view. Actually, the sun has stood where God has commanded it to stand since the moment He spoke it. It has never moved from its place in the sky and will only cease to shine when the will of God is fulfilled. The earth is the object that revolves around the sun, so no matter how we see it from man's perspective, God's spoken word solidifies His will. Isn't it a blessing to know that your life is predetermined by the will of God? Therefore, the magnitude of this single thought should reassure you that there is no need to walk in doubt or fear because nothing can hinder or prevent the will of God. Nothing that God has spoken into our lives can be impeded from coming to pass. The perfect will of God stands from the time He spoke it until He commands it to stop. That's just how awesome our God is! If He spoke it, it must come to pass and nothing or no one can stop it.

The will of God is perfect and God's desire is that man is fully aware of His will. God wants man to know His plan for His church. This is His universal will. It is also His desire that man knows His plan for His children. This is His individual will.

Likewise, He also wants us to be conscious of one important fact, and that is that He is supreme. So, ultimately, whether we consider His will perfect or permissive, God wants what He wants, and His will cannot be ignored.

When we take it all into perspective, some may ask the question: "How can I know what God wants?" or "Why doesn't He come down and tell us

Himself?" Well, the answer is simple. The Lord doesn't have an issue with making His will known, BUT we must be willing to listen when He does choose to disclose it to us. God has revealed in the scriptures how He communicates His will to the men and women who will HEAR Him. Clearly, through His word, we see three methods that God uses to assist us in understanding His will. The three methods involve Him speaking to us by visitation, revelation, and consolation.

APPLICATION EXERCISE:

The will of God is precise, so nothing happens in the believer's life by accident. In that hindsight is 20/20, write down five experiences that you encountered, that you later realized, were all a part of God's plan.

_____

_____

_____

_____

_____

_____

_____

_____

3

THE VISITATION

If we look back over the course of our lives, we will notice moments that God spoke to us even while we were totally out of His will. This alone disputes the mindset that many have, which suggests that "God doesn't hear a sinner's prayer." The truth is that it is the SINNER whom the Lord desires to talk to.

Through the Bible, we see examples of this truth. For instance, He spoke to the backslidden, Nation of Israel, through the Prophet Isaiah saying: "...come now and let us reason together, though your sins be as scarlet, I shall make them white like snow; though they be red as crimson, I shall make them as wool" (Isaiah 1:18, KJV).

For it is the sinner that is the one God visits, to reason with, and then, to turn this sinner to a saint. This conversation is the encounter with God that I call The Visitation. He reveals His will at the visitation. Yet, because we won't come to Him, except when we have something to say, our gracious and loving Father has decided to come to us.

As we experience this life's journey of its ups and downs, we walk daily from the cradle to the grave to establish who we are as a person. We allow our life experiences to shape and mold our thinking; not just our thinking concerning our world, but also our thinking concerning ourselves. Some say that we are a product of our environment, but once upon a time in an Era of Hip Hop someone said: "It isn't about where you're from, it's about where you're at." In other words, it's not the frame of your hood that shapes you, it's your frame of mind that shapes you.

Your experiences give you memories of moments that help you decide who you will become. This is where God intervenes in your experiences. For in experiences, your life is shifted by one visitation. The visitation is simply the divine intervention through an encounter with God.

For I am convinced that through divine interventions, that our God visits us from infancy to adulthood. In Matthew 18:10 (KJV), Jesus said of His little ones that: "…Their angels behold their Father's face both day and night." This alludes to the fact that in infancy, we have multiple encounters with our

Creator. For it is through these encounters, that we

become acquainted with His divine breath that fills us

with the essence of life.

When I consider the significance of this divine

breath, the word *zoe* comes to mind. *Zoe* originates

from the Hebrew language, and it is used to describe,

the life giving breath that was breathed into Adam.

The Bible teaches us that God breathed into Adam the

breath of life or *zoe* and that he became a living soul

(Genesis 2:7, KJV)." When we dig deeper for the meaning

of the word, we recognize that *zoe* is also defined as the

"Breath of Lives". Therefore at birth, God blew His breath

into our nostrils and our souls came alive.

In the infant's cry, there is a refreshing scent of the

breath of God. When the infant draws his or her first

breath, the first visitation as an earthly being is experienced. It is at this stage in life that God sends His angels, who resemble Him, to shine in His glory. As infants, we coo, smile, and laugh at their presence, while our parents assume that our expressions of joy are based solely on *their* presence. Oftentimes, they are oblivious to the fact that, as young babes, we are overjoyed to behold our Heavenly Father's face. Despite the fact that we rejoice as infants, a shift eventually takes place.

As we grow older, the fallen, Adamic nature overwhelms us and we lose that innate sensitivity to recognize His face and His voice. Our universal language that we all speak at birth is conformed to the sounds and syllables of those that care for us and we learn the language of men. Our sounds then mimic the voice of our environment and the familiar voice of God becomes foreign. As a result, we miss our visitation.

Fortunately, the Lord doesn't hold this against us because He already knows that as David said through God's prophetic utterance that: "We are born in sin and shaped in iniquity and in sin did our mothers conceive us" (Ps. 51:5, KJV). Through David, we come to the realization that this is where nature and nurture morph in us and blur our memory of our first moments of visitation. However, because of the Lord's love for us, He continues to make visitations until we reach the age of accountability; which most consider to be 12 years old. It is during this era of time that our decisions are no longer accredited to our ignorance. Instead, it is at the age of accountability that we are held liable for how we choose; whether

we choose good or evil. Despite the significance of

this age, the unyielding voice of God continues to call

in every language, in every dialect, and in every

tongue to every person saying: "I love you, my child"

(St. John 3:16, KJV), and "Come unto me, all ye that

labor and are heavy laden and I will give you rest…"

(Matthew 11:28, KJV).

This call that echoes in our spirit is to our

consciousness. The consciousness that we are asleep

to and lost to, must be awakened and can only be

awakened by the call or the voice of the sound of

God. The visitation is missed because we are more

conscious of our world than we are conscious of our

God.

In order to understand the essence of God's voice, we must also understand the concept of trichotomy.

Trichotomy suggests that we are a being made up of body, soul, and spirit. Through these three components of the human make-up, we become cognizant of the components that we are most accustomed to. Our bodies give us world-consciousness because it is accustomed to our world. Our soul gives us self-consciousness because it is the seat of our emotions and experiences. Our spirit gives us God-consciousness because it is the signature of our Creator.

Our body, gives us world-consciousness because our body connects us to our world. We become familiar with our world through our five

senses. Through the senses of touch, taste, sight,

smell, and hearing, we experience and become

conscious of our environment. This world, not the

world as in the earth but the systems of our world,

appeal to our fleshly or carnal desires. The world

pulls at our nature, our Adamic nature, that is prone

to sin. I John 2:15 (KJV) makes it a little clearer to

understand as John writes; "Do not love the world or

the things in the world. If anyone loves the world, the

love of the Father is not in him. "Verse 16 continues

"For all that is in the world, the lust of the flesh, the

lust of the eyes and the pride of life; is not of the

Father but is of the world." So, we struggle to obey

God because our bodies or our nature is drawn to

worldly lusts. This desire is not experience driven, it is instinctive in our nature and born into our DNA.

Beneath the exterior of our flesh or body is our soul. Our soul provides us with self–consciousness because our soul is the core of the natural man. The soul is the seat of our emotions and experiences. The soul is sometimes called the heart. This is not a reference to the internal organ that pumps blood through our bodies, but in this case, heart references the center or the core of our very being. The soul or the heart is the seat of our emotions and the residence of our core values and beliefs. Essentially, these emotions and core values/beliefs are vital because they aid in the construction of our personalities.

Ultimately, it is our soul which unites us to our true selves; that authentic you that only you and God know. Our soul is where our mind remembers the good and the bad. It is where we harbor who helped us and who hurt us. It is where we learn our behaviors, our likes, and our dislikes. In essence, our soul is the me that life made me. This is the me that God so loved (St. John 3:16, KJV).

Aside from the soul is our spirit, our human spirit which gives us a level of God–consciousness. In the Book of Romans, we learn that "Our spirit bears witness with His Spirit; that we are the sons of God" (Romans 8:16, KJV). The sin of Adam, through his disobedience and rebellion in the Garden of Eden by eating the forbidden fruit of The Tree of Good and

Evil, is the act that separated God's Spirit, which gave

Adam God-consciousness, from Adam's human spirit

which gave him self-consciousness. Adam lost his

innocence, while being awakened to his human

condition of nakedness and the Lord kicked Adam

and Eve out of the Garden. Our human spirit fell

with Adam's sin and we were born into that same

disobedient, rebellious, and sinful nature. In the end,

our world-consciousness pushed out the God nature

and left us stained with the Adamic rebellious nature.

Through this Adamic nature, we are empty of

the Zoe, "The Breath of Lives". We may even

consider this to be death in its rawest form. A death

that was triggered when the Lord told Adam, "…if

you disobey me, you will surely die" (Genesis 2:17,

KJV). After Adam's disobedience, he did not experience a physical death, but in that moment, his biological clock started ticking. His disobedience provoked a separation from zoe, the breath of God, and his human spirit, which introduced a form of death like none other.

Physical death is clearly understood as the separation of the spirit from the body. The body goes back to the dust from whence it came and the spirit returns to the God that gave it; while the soul (the heart, the mind, and the consciousness) spends eternity wherever judgement demands. Yet, the death that Adam experienced immediately prompted a spiritual death. That experience was the separation of the Spirit of God from the spirit of man. This left mankind blind to the God-consciousness that was gifted to us. This also left us blind to the Kingdom of God and deaf to the voice of God.

The danger of this blindness and deafness is recorded in St. John 3 (KJV) when Jesus spoke with Nicodemus. He clearly explained to him that if a person cannot see the Kingdom, nor will they enter into the kingdom without their spirit being reborn. Therefore, the Holy Ghost or Holy Spirit opens the eyes and ears of the child of God, so that their eyes and ears become sensitive to the vision and the voice of God. Through, this rebirthed sensitivity, we become reconnected with God, and once again become one with Him. This reacquaintance makes an allowance for His Spirit to merge with our spirit,

which creates a shift in the relationship.

Think of it as the relationship that Adam had

with God before breaking His command by indulging

in fruit from the Tree of the Knowledge of Good and

Evil. Can you envision Father and son walking

throughout the garden, conversing about Kingdom

matters and embracing the beauty of life in Eden?

Well, God desires that relationship with us. He

desires to commune closely with us and to walk with

us through the cool of our days. He longs to engage

us in conversations of purpose and power. In essence,

He simply longs for us to be in His presence. Through

the indwelling of the Holy Spirit, we can rest in His

presence. In His magnificent presence, He will speak

to us *if* we choose to listen. Yet, even if we choose not to listen, He will *still* speak to us.

In my unsaved life, the street life was all I knew, but I quickly came to a few realizations about God. He doesn't care where you are. He doesn't care about what hood you're from, what clique you're in, or your gang affiliation. He will come right where you are and allow you to experience a VISITATION. He's a faithful God!

Now, this is where the conversation begins with you and the will of God. The will of God has everything to do with the purpose of God for your life. It answers the question: "Why am I here?" The visitation answers the question: "God, what am I supposed to be doing?" The visitation will not always be a thunderous voice, but sometimes it can be heard

in the silence of a burning bush that gets your

attention. It can simply be a situation or circumstance

that makes you want to remove your shoes and bow

your head because you recognize your experience as a

move of God.

Regardless of the details of your visitation,

always remember that you don't want to miss the

Move of God in your life. God has been visiting us

since infancy, but our carnal minds and our love for

the world cry so loudly that they drown out the voice

of God from our ears. God can stand directly in our

face and we would still have no idea that He is there;

and before we know it we've missed the move.

In St. Luke's Gospel Chapter 24 (KJV), two of Jesus's disciples walked together on the road to Emmaus when Jesus appeared unto them. Despite the fact that these men were in close proximity to Jesus, verse 16 tells us that "But their eyes were holden that they should not know Him." Jesus was right there in their face, but they could not even recognize Him. How many of us can say that we've been these two men? Many times in our lives God was right there, but because He did not look the way we expected Him to look, we were blind to the occurrence of His visitation. We may have wanted Him to be tall, dark and handsome, but instead God looked very common or ordinary. We must keep in mind that God comes in the common to confound the complex. Sometimes the visitation is so common that we doubt that it is

God. We question the visitation by asking: "Where's the thunder?" and "Where's the lightning?" We miss him because of our carnal expectations.

You may recall that in I Kings 19:12 (KJV), the Prophet Elijah, fleeing for his life, entered a cave looking for direction from God. As he stepped onto the mountain, the great wind blew, but God was not in the wind. Then, the earthquake shook the mountain, but God was not in the earthquake. Then, a fire burned the mountain, but God was not in the fire. Then, in verses 12 and 13, the Bible tells us that after the fire, a still small voice was heard by Elijah.

The visitation of God doesn't meet our expectations because when God comes to speak to you concerning His will for your life, He comes in the common things that leave us standing in awe.

Let's also consider how Jesus spoke plainly in distaste to the Pharisees and Sadducees who were the religious leaders of His day. They would be our modern-day Preachers, Pastors, Reverends, Popes etc.… In St. Luke's Gospel 19:44 (KJV) it says, "And shall lay thee even with the ground, and thy children within thee; and they shall not leave in thee one stone upon another; BECAUSE THOU KNEWEST NOT THE TIME OF THY VISITATION." Whether we realize it or not, there are great consequences for missing our moments of a visitation from God.

Another example in the scriptures is of

Israel and how they lost their land to the Roman Empire, but they also lost their position with God by rejecting their visitation. You can miss God and you'll miss a life changing moment. You can miss God and you'll miss the difference between death and deliverance. You can miss God and you'll miss the difference between poverty and prosperity. You can miss God and you'll miss the difference between a break-up and a breakthrough. My point is that you can't afford to miss your visitation...no matter who you are or who you may think you're not in the sight of God.

As a teenager, I didn't really attend church regularly. So, imagine my surprise when I, had a visitation with God that altered the course of my life.

As a 16 or 17 year old teenager, growing up in the streets of Baltimore, Maryland, church and the will of God was the last thing on mind.

One day, I was walking home from what we called, "The Strip". In those days, I was filled with arrogance, which is how I coped with living a life of having to constantly look over my shoulder. This Saturday morning, as I walked home, the sun was beaming down on me in an unfamiliar way, but I didn't really notice at first because I was too busy watching my surroundings. In my mind, there was never a need for me to look up because all of the killers that I needed to be on the lookout for were on the ground level. So, as I walked and watched, I was contemplating the details of my day, when just for a slight moment, I glanced upward towards the sun. In

that moment, it was as if I became frozen in my

tracks. Immediately, I sobered up from the substances

that intoxicated my system from earlier, and stood in

awe of the crystal blue sky, the radiance of the sun

and the purity of the white clouds that drifted above

me. For the first time, I felt absolutely overwhelmed

by the celestial skies that hovered above me. The

magnificence of God's handiwork and His presence

brought this young thug to his knees in the middle of

the projects. I couldn't help but bow down and bask

in His glorious presence. I had never encountered

anything so powerful and humbling in my life. Yet,

moments later, I stood to my feet, stared at the

majestic scene above me and then dropped my head

in fear and shame.

In this moment, there was no lightning, no thunder, no mountain on fire, but I heard a still, small voice shatter the silence of that moment. No sound around me mattered because God had visited me. I can remember bowing my head again and saying: "Man, I don't know who you are; God, Jesus or whoever, but I know you're up there! I *know* you're real!"

On that particular day, I didn't give God my heart, but it was the beginning of a life of visitation after visitation after visitation.

The Bible says "The heavens declare the glory of God and the firmament shows His handiwork. (Psalms 19:1, KJV)" God didn't need lightning, thunder, or a mountain on fire to get my attention. All

He needed was for me to look up. All God needs for you to do, to get His will for your life downloaded into your spirit, is for you to look up.

Someone once said that "God doesn't hear a sinner's prayer", but that's not true. God is very attentive to the prayers of the lost soul. All He is waiting for is for the lost to whisper: "Help, me!" The visitation of God is designed for God to make a clear statement to the person He desires to communicate with. All He needs for us to do is to look up and say: "Show me your will for my life." Then, after this visitation, we get to know Him, recognize Him, and hear His voice.

Paul said, "that I might know Him, in the power of His resurrection and in the fellowship of His sufferings... (Phil. 3:10)" The visitation is God saying: "I know you and now it's time for you to know me."

In the 19th chapter of St. Luke's gospel, after Jesus's triumphal entry riding on a colt into Jerusalem, Jesus wept over the city saying: "...if thou had known, even thou, at least in this thy days, the things which belong unto thy peace! But now they are hid from thine eyes. ...because thou knewest not the time of thy VISITATION" (Luke 19:44, KJV). Israel as a nation had no idea of who was standing before them. God incarnate, their LORD, their King and Deliverer. Jehovah Himself had come down, in the face of Jesus Christ to visit His children and they treated Him like a common carpenter's son. Israel's treatment of Jesus is indicative of a missed visitation.

They made the mistake that many of us make. Since Jesus didn't look like, sound like, or act like they EXPECTED their Messiah to look, sound or act they disregarded Him. The lesson to be learned here is that God will not always come to us in the way that you expect Him to. We may not be familiar with how He chooses to visit with us, but in the end, we must be open to His voice.

Jesus said to Israel that, because of them missing their visitation that their enemies would annihilate them. In like manner, if we miss our visitation, then the enemy will have an opportunity to get the upper hand in our lives. If we miss the visitation, the enemy will attempt to annihilate us just like the Children of Israel. If we miss our visitation, we miss the move of God. If we miss our visitation, we miss the will of God for our lives. In essence, missing our visitation may cause us to lose everything including our lives. Not knowing the visitation of God and not knowing the Voice of God, gives the enemy the time to take our lives before we can even live. When it's all said and done, we must understand that we cannot afford to miss our visitation. There is too much at stake.

So, remember that when Heaven opens and touches earth, it behooves us to listen. My visitation was God saying to me, "I love you even though I know how bad you are. I opened Heaven to let you know that I've got my eyes on you." God came to me, a nobody and showed Himself to me in the beauty of the sky. It's the same sky that He spoke into

existence in the first chapter of Genesis, but this time

it was as a visitation.

As you dive deeper into this book, please note

that understanding the will of God comes by *many*

visitations, encounters, and experiences with Him.

From the cradle to the grave, He'll keep coming to

help us to understand that this experience is not luck

or fortune, but it's God. He wants you to know that

He sees all that you are going through and that He

hasn't forgotten about you. He wants you to know

that He is not willing to wait on you to get yourself

together; as we often say. He's coming to you just the

way you are; reeking of alcohol, patronizing a local

bar, or resting in the midst of depression and

discouragement. Regardless of where you are

physically, mentally, emotionally, or spiritually, He is

coming to meet you right where you are.

He comes to us for one simple, yet very

profound reason. He loves us. The depths of His love

runs so deeply that He wants us to know that He is

here to help us through this life; but, only if we allow

Him to. The visitation that we encounter is propelled

by this love that seeks to disrupt our plans, dreams,

and goals, so that His divine will can be interjected.

Initially, we may not appreciate His love, and

heed to His voice right away, but the more He visits

us the louder His voice becomes; the more His love

for us becomes more evident, and the more our

spiritual ears will be able to recognize His voice more

clearly. If we can listen to His voice, then we can experience our visitation.

Take a moment to consider Samuel. Samuel was a great prophet of God, yet he did not recognize his first visitation. In the book of I Samuel 3:1 (KJV), after Samuel was "…lent to the Lord…" by his mother, Hannah, he grew up under the care of the High Priest. Hannah was the wife of Elkanah who loved her dearly, but she could not have a child. Hannah would not give up so easily, she went to the Temple and wept to the Lord for a child. Eli, the priest of that day told her that the Lord heard her prayer and she was impregnated by her husband shortly thereafter. She promised the Lord that if He answered her prayer that she would give the child back to Him. She named the child Samuel meaning "lent to the Lord" and after weaning the child, she took him back to the temple and gave him to Eli, the High Priest, to serve in the Lord's house.

Now, you may recall that under Eli's spiritual leadership, Israel's relationship with God became strained because of their evil deeds. In the text, the scripture said "…that there was no open vision and ere (almost) the lamp of God had gone out…" (I Samuel 3:3, KJV). This means that during this time that Jehovah had grown silent. He wasn't speaking to Eli, which meant that He also wasn't speaking to the nation. Yet, the text continued by saying: "…and the Lord called Samuel… and he ran to Eli and asked him did he call him and Eli said: "No, I did not call you…"

(I Samuel 3:5, KJV). The Lord called Samuel three times and each time Samuel ran to Eli and Eli assured him that he had not call him. The Bible said that Samuel did not yet know the voice of the Lord (I Samuel 3:7, KJV). The Lord called Samuel, but he did not recognize His voice.

What we can glean from this text is that, in some visitations, the Lord will speak to us, but in a voice that sounds familiar to us. To not miss your visitation, you must listen closely because familiar sounds may carry the voice of God. Samuel may have been hearing the Lord's call but in Eli's voice. The story ends with the young Samuel being called a fourth time, and just like before, he ran to Eli again. However, this time Eli said, "I perceive that the Lord is calling you" (I Samuel 3:8, KJV). So, Eli instructed

Samuel, when you hear the call again say: "…Here I

am Lord". After receiving this direct instruction from

Eli, Samuel grew to learn how to recognize the voice

of the Lord *and* how to obey it.

Since Samuel's day, things have remained the

same in that sense that God is still talking to His

people. However, the question to be pondered is *if*

*God is **still** talking or we listening?* Samuel had to learn

the voice of the Lord, and once he did, he became the

prophet of his nation. We cannot afford to miss our

day of visitation because we may be the familiar voice

of God that someone needs to hear to experience their

breakthrough.

Think about the moments that you heard the voice of God, either in the glory of a bright, blue sky or the wonder of a falling star. Or maybe your moment may have been in a familiar voice calling: "HEY, it's the LORD "or a still small voice that speaks quietly in your heart. It may be mama's voice or daddy's voice or grandmother's voice simply because God speaks through the familiar, so it may sound like someone familiar, but it's God talking to you. Whatever your experience, the Lord visits the saints and the sinners for a purpose. The visitation is to reveal the will of God to the believer, to bring revelation to the Samuels, Abrahams and Daniels of our day. Understanding the will of God is recognizing when God visits you and the purpose of that visit. The VISITATION is the open door for the

REVELATION.

4

THE REVELATION

When seeking to understand the will of God for your life, it is good to begin at the visitation. We cannot afford to miss our day of visitation, because it is the day that we see God. If we really think back over our lives, we may realize that God has come to visit us in our past. Yet, we've missed our visitation. We missed it because we were focused on the physical, the natural, and the carnal. We ran to Eli, as Samuel did, because the voice sounded familiar. Yet, the answers that we sought weren't in the sound of the familiar voices of those around us. We don't always recognize that God is talking to us. Nevertheless, it is a wonderful thing to know that God loves us so much

that He continuously returns to the door of our hearts

and persists on knocking. When we choose to open

the door, we then see the face of God revealed in

Jesus Christ. At this point, it doesn't even matter what

God sounds like or what He looks like. All that truly

matters is that you know that you're in the presence

of the Living God. So, to acknowledge His presence,

we bow down and show reverence like many men

and women did in the days of old.

When we experience the presence of God, we

know that He hasn't shown up to have tea and

cookies, but instead, He comes with a divine purpose

in mind. With this in mind, we become enlightened.

Our eyes are opened, and we realize that we are

smack dab in the middle of a visitation. The need to hear God now is major because no visitation is for naught. The visitation occurs to reveal the will of God to His people. Within this moment of revelation, God provides answers for our individual situations and circumstances. However, as Christians, we must believe that by faith, that the God of all creation loves us enough to intervene in the events that happen in our everyday lives. The Lord wants to inform us of His perfect plans and purpose for our lives. The scriptures declare to us that thus says the Lord, "… my people are destroyed for lack of knowledge…" (Hosea 4:6, KJV). If we don't know what God wants, then how can we operate in His will? The destruction of a nation is not dependent upon its gross domestic product or GDP, it's military might, or the destructiveness of its nuclear weapons, but a nation's destruction is dependent upon their failure to remember and reverence our great and mighty God.

As believers, we must be equipped with the knowledge that directs us to the Kingdom, so who better to impart this knowledge than the King of the Kingdom? We don't want to miss God when He starts talking. When God speaks, cosmos are formed and knowledge is revealed. So, the knowledge of God is not limited to the laws of theology but God reveals Himself and His will to His servants by revelation.

Despite the fact that the word revelation, should be honored and valued by God's people, it is often met with great fear and intimidation. When most people hear the word revelation, they only envision the Book of the Bible that speaks of beast and

dragons; demons and angels, wars and witches.

Indeed, the Book of Revelations does reveal the final

conflict of the Lord God, His Christ and the Kingdom.

Yet, Jesus made it clear that whoever reads the Book

of Revelations is blessed (Revelations 1:3, KJV), so the

book is not to be feared. The Book of Revelations

should be respected and highly regarded as the

unveiling of the universal will of God, which is God's

will for everyone. However, this does not exclude the

fact that revelation also comes to us relative to His

individual will for each of us. Regardless of whether

it's His universal will or His individual will, the truth

of the matter is that both come through the revelation

of God.

Let's continue delving into this subject matter by studying the meaning of revelation. The word revelation in its Greek context is the word *APOKALYPSIS*, which is simply interpreted to mean to unveil or to reveal (Strong, Kohlenberger, & Swanson, 2001). Revelation in more layman terms refers to God opening the eyes of the spiritually blind in an effort to cause us to see His divine will. It's the unveiling, as if God exposes His purpose or pulls the cover off of a gift that you couldn't see in plain sight. God wants you in "the know". In other words, through revelation God gives you knowledge and understanding because God is not pleased with His children living their lives in ignorance. He comes in a visitation to give us revelation for our situations.

When God speaks, it's clean, crisp and relevant. His words bring clarity and understanding. His words help us to make sense of the nonsense that attempts to drive us out of the will of God, to drive us out of the way of God, and to drive us out of our minds.

The Word of God comes to make sure you and I don't lose our minds. Without revelation we wouldn't know, without knowing we would have no word, without a word from God we would lose our minds in the mayhem of life.

So, for this, we must thank God for a word. "His word is a lamp unto our feet and a light unto our pathway (Psalms 119:105, KJV)." For without His word we wouldn't have a guiding light to help us maneuver through this obstacle course of life. We would fail to have a shining light in the darkest times of our lives. Remember that He said: "His word will not return unto Him void, but it will accomplish that which He pleases (Isaiah 55:11, KJV)." God's word is not void or empty, but it is perfect, complete, and precise. He said, I have spoken it and I will also bring it to pass; I have purposed it, I will also do it" (Isaiah 46:9-11). The perfect will of God is unstoppable, irreversible, and immutable. Even if man refuses to live in the perfect will of God, what God willed will still come to pass. If God makes a visitation and imparts revelation and you or I refuse His perfect will for our lives, God will still have a willing soul to do what He asked. You and I, in our rebellion, will simply miss the move of God. The Apostle Paul made it very clear in Romans 9:13 – 23 (KJV) that we can't fight against the will of God even when others ask the question "… who hath resisted His will?" (Rom. 9:19, KJV). The answer will always be no one. God's will must come to pass regardless if I want it to or not. We may not want the revelation of the will of God, however, we sure cannot stop it. This is the assurance to every believer that regardless of who voted you out, they can't stop you. Regardless of your haters, you can't be stopped. Even if the devil comes with a blizzard, God will bring a snow blower and bring you out in a snow mobile. My point is that the revelation of God is life changing and if you are in the will of God, then you're unstoppable; nor can you ever be defeated.

The key to achieving this unstoppable and

undefeated lifestyle is connected to your ability to

humble yourself to His voice.

Always remember that when God starts

talking to you, that your job, as His son or daughter,

is just to listen closely with your heart and to receive

every drop. Don't take for granted the fact that when

revelation comes from God that He may say it once

but you will hear it over and over in your spirit. This

is confirmed in Psalms 62:11 (KJV) when the writer

pens: "Once has He said it, twice have you heard it."

The significance of this scripture encourages us to

allow the word to resonate in our spirit and to hold

fast to it as though it was just spoken to us. This is so

pertinent in the life of a believer because God's word

is not echoed in your ear for nothing. No, the Word will echo into your ear and down into your heart, so that it can guide you into your destiny. Your destiny is not the end of your journey, but it *IS* the journey. Minute by minute, decade by decade, experience after experience, God walks us through a life filled with the ups and downs of not just living, but living a life full of abundance (St. John 10:10, KJV).

This abundance that we all seek is contrived through our ability to hear the Word of God. For the Bible tells us that we should "be swift to hear, slow to speak and slow to wrath" (James 1:19, KJV). Learning to listen is the key to revelation. As a people, it is engrained in our nature to be quick to speak and slow to listen. We make the mistake of spending too much time asking God for our desires and attempting to explain to Him what *our* will is. Yet, we fail to understand that it is so much easier to hear God when our mouths are shut. It's ironic how we make something so simple so much more complex than what God intended for it to be. All we need to do is to open our spiritual ears and we'll begin to hear His voice.

As I reflect on the principle of closing our mouths and opening our spiritual ears, I'm reminded of a visitation where God gave me revelation. I was considering moving from my hometown of Baltimore, Maryland to Sumter, South Carolina. To those around me the idea of moving during this season of my life was asinine. It was at this stage in my life where things were going considerably well for me. I was

serving in a great ministry, holding a management

position on my job, and had recently purchased a new

home. Things were truly looking up for my family

and I. Then, out of nowhere, God interrupted my

norm by speaking four little words: "It's time to

move." Of course, hearing the voice of God was not

foreign to me at this point, but this time, His directive

totally blindsided me, and frankly, I wasn't in

agreement. So, as many of us do, I sought clarity by

going on a fast and by seeking God through prayer. I

was in search of clarity, but one false move could

have easily pushed me outside of His will. However,

interestingly enough, that week I received a call from

my boss. He informed me that I had been

recommended for a promotion and that all I needed

to do to receive it was to respond in the affirmative. This was exciting news, and I was tempted by his offer. Instead, I decided to delay giving a hasty response, and to continue fasting and praying. Shortly after receiving this offer from my boss, I received yet another offer.

Within that same week I received an offer to build my ministry. This time the offer came in the form of a phone call from my pastor. As one of his members, over the years, we had developed a good relationship. I looked to him for his spiritual guidance, wisdom, and mentorship. I respected him greatly, and was honored when he asked me to serve in a pastoral role at one of his three churches. Of course, in my mind, I wanted to believe that this was a great reason not to make the move. This was an opportunity to minister to God's people at a greater level, so, again, I found myself feeling tempted to stay even though God had said to go.

Now, with both offers on the table, I asked myself *Why move to another state when my financial situation is about to change for the better? Why move to another state when I'm about to become a pastor of a growing church and receive a salary?* Eventually, I came to the conclusion that my boss's offer was good, but the pastor's offer was definitely too good not to be God. After hearing my pastor's offer, I was convinced that God had changed His mind.

That night, after leaving Bible Study, I went home and started watching Christian Television. I was in search of confirmation, when one of my favorite preachers came on the screen. He peered into the camera and said: "Someone is about to make you an offer you can't refuse. Refuse it!" At that moment, I immediately begin to weep and to repent for my rebellious thinking. I was no fool. I knew that the Bible says "Once has He said it, twice have you heard it; the power belongs to God" (Ps. 62:11, KJV). The Lord didn't have to tell me a third time; besides, I don't think He was going to say it again.

My point in sharing this experience was to remind you that sometimes what looks good to you may not be good for you.

When I was growing up, they used to tell me that everything that glitters isn't gold. Definitely what we see looks appealing to the flesh, but it isn't always what it seems. Most times it isn't authentic. It isn't genuine, and if you choose it over the real thing, then there's a price to pay in the end. What we see is tempting, but it has no real value. We see this clearly in the encounter that Jesus had with Satan.

In Matthew 4, the devil offered Jesus the wealth of the world in exchange for Him bowing down and worshipping him, but Jesus refused and replied "...get thee hence Satan; for it is written, Thou shalt worship the Lord thy God and Him only shalt thou serve" (Matthew 4:10, KJV). In this instance, we see how the devil tried to offer Jesus comfort. Comfort is gratifying but it requires that you bow down and sell the most valuable asset that you have which is your soul. In contrast, please know that the will of God is not always comfortable. In fact, the will of God usually will wreck your plans, disrupt your dreams, and invade your comfort zone. When God begins to speak to you and reveal His will, He'll push you out of the familiar like He did Abraham. He will command you to go. Go to your next level. Go across the country. Go get your blessing.

At times, it's frustrating to hear the command "Go", and it can be even more frustrating when there's no divine explanation either. The Lord doesn't always explain your journey to you step by step. If He did, we would try to talk ourselves out of everything that God is trying to talk us into.

Stop trying to talk yourself out of what God is trying to talk you into. Listen for the revelation and be like Abraham and obey the voice of God. Make the decision to "walk by faith and not by sight" (II Corinthians 5:7, KJV). This way of thinking opposes everything that society teaches us about connecting with the world around us. Society instructs us to see a thing so that we can believe in it. On the other hand, God's way teaches us that seeing is not believing but that believing is seeing. This is confirmed throughout the scriptures. For example, Romans 8:24 (KJV) says "…for what a man can see, why would he hope for it?" (Romans 8:24, KJV).

In essence, allow God to stretch you beyond the break. The break is the place you stopped. The break is the place beyond your comfort zone. The break is where the devil drew a line in the sand and told you that you could only go but so far. This challenge from the enemy is to stop you dead in your tracks. He is threatened by the thought of you experiencing a divine revelation as a result of your obedience.

It is imperative to remember that revelation from the Lord to His child sets in motion the individual will of God for that individual, which whom He speaks to. God wants so much more for us. He desires for us to reach our full potential and to fulfill His divine purpose. So, this is not the time to listen to the people that don't believe in you or don't believe that God spoke to you. Now is not the time to listen to the people that say: "You can't do that. "You

shouldn't do that." Or "I wouldn't do that if I were

you." Whatever you do, don't allow people to talk

you out of the will of God. Although, He may not tell

you everything, what He does tell you, obey with all

your might; because His revelation comes to keep you

in the will of God.

Hence, the word *will,* from Philippians 4 is the

Greek word **Thelema**. The word Thelema is defined as

"the will, the decision, the desire or the pleasure of

God" (Strong et al., 2001). Ultimately, we should want

God's will for our lives. We should want the Lord to

make the decisions that guide our lives. In reality,

when we want what God wants for our lives, then we

desire to experience His good pleasure. This is why

the scripture tells the believer to "fear not little flock,

for it is your Fathers good pleasure to give you the

Kingdom" (Luke 12:32, KJV). Jesus is King of kings.

He's King of the Kingdom and He loves us so much

that He has made us partakers of His Great Kingdom.

Revelation from God reveals the will, the

decision, the desire, and the pleasure that God has

ordained for our lives. This revelation moves us from

the carnal realm to the Kingdom realm by

empowering us with spiritual knowledge. Knowing is

empowering, while ignorance is paralyzing. As a

result, people would rather be ignorant, than to be

held accountable to know the desire of God. They

assume that what they don't know won't hurt them.

Yet, the exact opposite is actually the truth. What you

don't know can kill you! Ignorance of the will of God

for your life is like having sight but walking through life with your eyes closed. If you did that, you would miss so many beautiful moments that God desires to reveal to you.

The scripture says that "…Eye hath not seen, nor ear heard, neither have entered into the heart of man, the things which God hath prepared for them that love Him." But, don't stop there, the scripture goes on to say; "But God hath *revealed* them unto us by His Spirit" (I Corinthians 2: 9 – 10, KJV). What your eyes haven't seen, what your ears haven't heard and the things that haven't even entered your heart, God has prepared and wants to reveal or impart revelation to those that love Him. He wants you to know His will for your life because He has so many wonderful things in store for His sons and daughters. As much as we've fallen and gone astray, regardless of the several mistakes that we've made, He still has so many wonderful things prepared. The Lord is not shocked by our mistakes, our bad judgements, or our missed opportunities to give Him glory. The Lord has predetermined our purpose and has prepared for our failures. The will of God is so perfect that the devil himself will have to bow to the King of all kings and the Lord of all lords: Jesus Christ. The will of God is that, man bows now or he will bow later.

Jesus prayed in what we refer to as The Lord's Prayer "…thy Kingdom come, thy will be done in earth, as it is in Heaven" (Matthew 6:10, KJV). The perfect will of God is all about one King, establishing one Kingdom. That as the Lord resides, rules, and

reigns in Heaven, so shall He do the same on earth.

Heaven doesn't resist, reject, or rebel against the will

of God; but makes herself subject, subservient and

submissive to His will. The earth is in chaos,

confusion and rebellion, and must yield in obedience

to the Lord God Almighty. Since Heaven is His

throne and the Earth is His footstool, then it is proper

for that which is under His feet be found under His

rule. The Lord has never stopped reigning, He is just

the Master of a master plan to make the Kingdom of

God and the kingdom of men one kingdom. He is the

Master Chess player. He strategically moves the seen

and the unseen in order to align everything with His

purpose and to reveal His perfect will. Paul refers to

God's perfect will in Romans 12:2 (KJV) when he

admonishes the believer to "…be ye transformed by

the renewing of your mind, that you might prove

what that good and acceptable and perfect will of

God." Engaging in the Father's perfect will occurs

when a metamorphosis engages that shifts the

believer's mind from carnal to kingdom.

Fundamentally, an indicator of one's revelation of the

perfect will of God is evidenced by an altered

thinking pattern. Whereas at one time things

associated with your carnality made sense, now

things associated with God's Kingdom are the only

things that make sense to you. Through, the

revelation of His will, you begin to acknowledge that

life is no longer aligning with things that make good

sense, but now you choose to align with things that

make "God sense". This means that your thinking

changes for a purpose, and this purpose is that you might prove what is that good, acceptable and perfect will of God (Romans 12:2, KJV).

As we closely examine the meaning of this scripture, we noticed that God's will can be revealed at various levels. The first level is considered "the good". This "good will" is considered to be honorable in nature. It pushes the believer in a place to honor the word and the will of God. It results in the believer making changes and adjustments that prove his or her allegiance to the Kingdom.

The "acceptable will" is what is well pleasing, acceptable, and fully agreeable with the Word of God. The believer is fully in agreement with the word of God and has willingly accepted the universal purpose and plan of God. This is possibly where saving faith connects the believer to salvation.

Lastly, the perfect will is what is the finished, full grown, and mature performance of the word of God. It seeks to fulfill the personal will of God in the believer's life. The perfect will of God is the believer stepping onto the water of destiny and walking in the purpose of God. God can reveal His will immediately to you but you will not receive the whole roll all at once. Instead, you receive His will "... line upon line and precept upon precept, here a little there a little..." (Isaiah 28:10, KJV). In other words, revelation comes in process: good, acceptable and perfect.

The will of God is spoken to us through the Word of God. The word of God will never fail but it will accomplish what the Lord has sent it to do. The Lord spoke the "logos" or the word uttered by His voice to create something out of nothing (Strong et al., 2001). That's what He does with our lives. He speaks into a heart void and empty and like the sun, moon and stars; then, joy, peace and love instantly appear. That same logos that created was made flesh through Jesus Christ. Jesus touched, healed and delivered us that we may know His will for our lives. God speaks loudest through His word because it is "quick (living), powerful (authoritative), sharper than any two – edged sword…"(Hebrews 4:12, KJV). The living word shuts the mouth of doubt and fear and speaks life into our darkest places and the light shines out of the darkness. Through this light, our dead hearts shine with the purpose that He planned for us.

In the end, the closer we draw to the word of God, the closer our ears are to hearing His voice. The more we hear His voice the greater our revelation. The greater our revelation, the more we walk in the perfect will of God. When we feel that we have no idea of what the Lord is attempting to reveal to us, the entrance of His word giveth light and we will know what the will of the Lord is for us.

5

THE CONSOLATION

The trouble with not knowing the will of God is that uncertainty, insecurity, and doubt will cause you to feel like you're walking around in circles. The Israelites were delivered out of the slavery of Egypt with liberty, wealth, and a promise from God to inherit a blessing. Yet, after seeing the miracles of God, from sending Egypt into bankruptcy, to opening the Red Sea and allowing them to walk over on dry land, the people complained because of the harsh terrain of the wilderness. They allowed these challenges to persuade them to believe that life would be better in Egypt. They desired to return to the bondage that God had just delivered them from. They just couldn't see the blessing that was in store for

them on the other side of their wilderness. By the

same token, we often operate with a similar mindset

when we have no clue about how God is going to

bring us out of our situations. We stand at the edge of

the wilderness crying out to God and demand that He

tells us step by step what we will face in our

wilderness. Nevertheless, we fail to accept the fact

that if God told us everything we would encounter on

our way to the promise land, that we would try to

modify the will of God. We would respond like Israel

and wander in the wilderness for 40 years when God

only intended for the trip to take 40 days. Our

response, like Israel, is associated with not knowing

every move of God. This "not knowing" mindset can

cause feelings of anxiety, but if we rely on God's

revelation, then it is enough to bring consolation to our souls.

We are reminded of this in Hebrews 6:8 (KJV) when the scripture says: "That by two immutable things, in which it was impossible for God to lie, we might have a strong consolation, who have fled for refuge to lay hold upon the hope set before us..." (Heb. 6:8, KJV). In the original Greek text, the word consolation is interpreted from the word *paraklesis* which means solace, comfort, consolation and refreshment (Strong et al., 2001).

After the visitation, comes revelation, but after the revelation, we have to be willing to wait on the promise of God to manifest. Therefore, God sends consolation, comfort, solace and a refreshing so that we won't go back to the bondage that He delivered us from. God doesn't want us to give up in the fight because things get tough, or because it doesn't look like what God said. The Lord comes and sits down on the edge of the bed with you and wraps His fatherly arms around you as you scream, pray and cry. He lovingly whispers in your ear that everything will end victoriously. He comforts you and tells you that you're going to make it. He reminds you that "... all things are working for your good..." (Rom. 8:28, KJV). Regardless of how dark and uncertain moments in your life become, the Lord will meet you there because He's promised that He'll "never leave you, neither will He forsake you" (Heb. 13:5, KJV). Never forget that God doesn't care where you are because all He wants is you.

While at your lowest state, you don't understand the will of God and you feel like you're going to lose your mind. However, it is critical that you don't lose it in these moments. The believer can't afford to lose their mind between the promise and the blessing. That's what can change the entire will of God for our lives. That's why the consolation of God is vital to our survival because the visitation and the revelation is in jeopardy if we don't have the strength for the journey to the promise.

When God sends comfort our tears cease, our anxiety calms, our fear flees, and we're filled with the peace of God. It is the peace of God that keeps our minds. " For the peace of God, which passes all understanding; shall keep your hearts and minds through Christ Jesus" (Phil. 4:7, KJV).

God's remedy for our depression is the peace of God. The will of God never demands for us to figure everything out, but the will of God demands for us to simply trust Him. This trust will encourage us to rely on God whole-heartedly and "to lean not to our own understanding, but in all thy ways acknowledge Him, so that He can direct our paths" (Pro. 3: 5-6, KJV)." Throughout our life, we must accept that our understanding is faulty. It can take us in a 40 year circle where we deal with the same devil on a different day instead of entering our land of promise. So, instead of resting our destinies on our own understanding, we must believe that God knows exactly what He's doing as He directs every phase of our lives. Overall, we must acknowledge that the good is working for our good and the bad is working for our good. Whatever He allows us to go through is working for us.

In spite of what we face, we should choose the mindset of the Apostle Paul in Romans 5:38 (KJV) when He proclaimed that He gloried in tribulation. For Paul understood that tribulation works patience and patience experience and experience hope and hope does not make us ashamed." When you're in the will of God, He knows all about your tribulation. He knows all about your trouble. He knows all about your wilderness, so whatever you face is working for you and not against you.

The Word tells us that "Ye have need of patience, that after you have done the will of God that you may obtain the promise" (Heb. 10:36, KJV). So, keep in mind that consolation comes to comfort us while you wait for God to bring His promise to pass. "Our promise is coming, but we must "Wait on the Lord and be of good courage and He shall strengthen our heart" (Ps. 27:14, KJV).

Consolation from God is giving us strength and courage right now. He wants us to know that we are in His will. For His will is perfect so we couldn't be in a safer place. Through our consolation, God catches our tears in a bottle (Ps. 58:8, KJV) and in the process of time, wipes them all away. The consolation is that you may not understand it all but the visitation and revelation made things just a little bit clearer; that we're not in this fight alone but Jesus is fighting with and for us.

Ultimately, what we know is that we encounter one visitation after another, one revelation after another, and one time of comfort after another. Living in the will of God is not just any kind of life, but it is a life of expectation and celebration. Understanding the will of God is the assurance of knowing that purpose and destiny are on the other side of our pain. It is an assurance in knowing that our labor is not in vain, but it will bring forth the promise of God. It is also the assurance of knowing that everyone that walked away did so for a divine purpose and that everyone who stayed, stayed

because they share in that purpose.

So, commit to embarking upon life's journey

with expectation, determination and motivation. For

these are the necessary keys to gaining an

understanding of God's will for our lives, so that we

may fully embrace our divine purpose.

REFERENCES

Knowledge. (2013). Webster's All-In-One Dictionary

& Thesaurus (5th ed.) Springfield, MA: Federal

Street Press.

Perfect. (2013). Webster's All-In-One Dictionary &

Thesaurus (5th ed.) Springfield, MA: Federal

Street Press.

Strong, J., Kohlenberger, J.R., and Swanson, J.A.

(2001). *The stronget strong's exhaustive*

concordance of the bible. Grand Rapids,

Michigan: Zondervan.

Made in the USA
Columbia, SC
03 February 2018